Raintree is an imprint of Capstone Global Library Limited, a company incorporated in England and Wales having its registered office at 7 Pilgrim Street, London, EC4V 6LB – Registered company number: 6695582

www.raintreepublishers.co.uk
myorders@raintreepublishers.co.uk.

Edited by Andrew Farrow, Adam Miller, and Adrian Vigliano
Designed by Richard Parker
Original illustrations © HL Studios
Illustrated by James Stayte (pages 4–7); HL Studios
Picture research by Ruth Blair
Production by Sophia Argyris
Originated by Capstone Global Library Ltd
Printed and bound in China by CTPS

ISBN 978 1 406 26104 2 (hardback)
17 16 15 14 13
10 9 8 7 6 5 4 3 2 1

ISBN 978 1 406 26110 3 (paperback)
18 17 16 15 14
10 9 8 7 6 5 4 3 2 1

British Library Cataloguing in Publication Data
Spilsbury, Richard
Health and disease : investigating a TB outbreak. – (Anatomy of an investigation)

A full catalogue record for this book is available from the British Library.

Acknowledgements

We would like to thank the following for permission to reproduce photographs: Alamy p. 12 (© Custom Medical Stock Photo); Corbis pp. 11 (© Corbis), 15 (© David Snyder/ZUMA Press), 47 (© Carlos Cazalis); Getty Images pp. 13 (Jose Luis Pelaez Inc), 16 (Matt McClain for The Washington Post), 21 (Karen Kasmauski), 21 (Spencer Platt), 25 (Workbook Stock), 29 (SSPL), 39 (Chris Hondros), 40 (Dan Kitwood), 41 (Cultura/Peter Muller), 47 (Peter Parks/AFP); Science Photo Library pp. 8 (Eye of Science), 17 (Prof. S.H.E. Kaufmann & Dr J.R Golecki), 18 (Mark Thomas), 22 (Andy Crump, TDR, WHO), 30 (BSIP, Laurent, Maya), 33 (Elisabeth Schneider/Look at Sciences), 38 (Henn Photography), 43 (A. Crump, TDR, WHO); Shutterstock pp. 21 (© f9photos), 26 (© Lisa F. Young), 49 (© hxdbzxy); Superstock pp. 23 (Medical RF), 24 (William Radcliffe), 37 (imagebroker.net); WHO p. 35 (Nick Otto).

Cover photograph reproduced with permission of Corbis (© Andrew Brookes).

We would like to thank David Wright for his invaluable help in the preparation of this book.

Every effort has been made to contact copyright holders of any material reproduced in this book. Any omissions will be rectified in subsequent printings if notice is given to the publisher.

Disclaimer

All the internet addresses (URLs) given in this book were valid at the time of going to press. However, due to the dynamic nature of the internet, some addresses may have changed, or sites may have changed or ceased to exist since publication. While the author and publisher regret any inconvenience this may cause readers, no responsibility for any such changes can be accepted by either the author or the publisher.

Health and Disease:
INVESTIGATING A TB OUTBREAK

Richard Spilsbury

Contents

Some words are printed in bold, **like this**. You can find out what they mean by looking in the glossary on page 52.

COUGHING FITS

The Easter holiday is over, and now final exams are looming. Jack is taking the tube home

Jack's mum is still worried, but she's hoping he will get better in time for his exams.

But Jack starts to feel worse. He is not sleeping well and is lacking energy. Plus, he has that bad cough...

Look what you've done, Jack, coughing so hard!

...and he's found blood in his tissue.

Please get the doctor to come as soon as possible – he just doesn't seem well.

Cough...

It looks like Jack does not have pneumonia after all, and that it might be tuberculosis (TB). If so, this is bad news, because he could have spread the disease to his family, friends, and other people he has come into contact with. It is time to start a full investigation...

Investigating disease

Have you ever heard of **tuberculosis (TB)**? If so, you probably know that it is a disease. A disease is something that stops your body from functioning normally, such as an **infection** you catch from someone or something you cannot pass on, like cancer. This book is about TB and the detective work people carry out to find out who has this **infectious disease**, how they got it, and how to stop other people from getting it.

The danger of TB

TB usually causes damage to the lungs, although it can also affect other organs. The infection causes the **tissue** to grow differently and to die if untreated. When people's lungs do not work properly, they cough a lot and find it difficult to breathe. Many infectious diseases are caused by **micro-organisms** (tiny living things) getting into the body and growing or living there. TB is no different. It is caused by a particular species, or type, of **bacteria** called *Mycobacterium tuberculosis*.

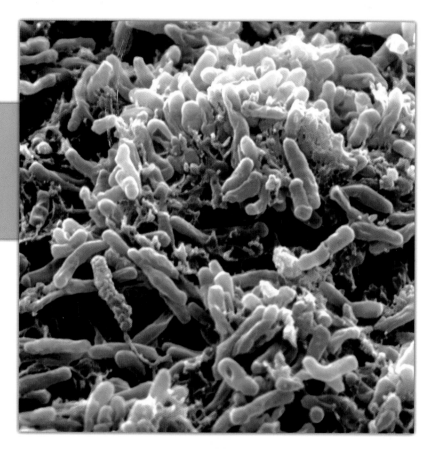

The pathogen causing TB infection in millions of people worldwide is very tiny. Around 400 of these end to end would fit on a pinhead.

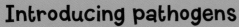

Introducing pathogens

We commonly use the word *germs* to describe the things that cause diseases and infections, but a more correct term is **pathogens**. Have you ever had athlete's foot? That is caused by a fungal pathogen, meaning it is caused by something called a fungus. Many bacteria are pathogens. They are tiny living organisms, and billions of them exist globally. What about coughs and sneezes? The likely culprit for these is a pathogen called the cold **virus**. Viruses are up to 100 times smaller than bacteria, and they are only active if they are inside a living cell of another organism.

All viruses are harmful, but many bacteria are good for us. For example, some bacteria that live in the intestines help us digest food. But the pathogenic bacteria that infect our bodies can cause anything from sore throats to infected cuts, the disease meningitis, and TB.

The six deadliest infectious diseases

In many **developing countries**, pathogens are major killers. This is partly because many people in these countries cannot afford healthcare or they have limited access to it. It is partly because not enough people are available to investigate disease outbreaks and prevent their spread. It is also the result of poor education about how diseases spread. Six pathogens in particular affect billions of people and kill millions each year.

Disease	Type of pathogen	Number infected	Approximate number of deaths per year
Pneumonia	Bacteria	>150 million	>2 million
TB	Bacteria	2 billion	1.5 million
Diarrhoea	Bacteria/protozoa/other	1.5 billion	2 million
Malaria	Protozoa	275 million (approx.)	1 million
Measles	Virus	20 million	140,000
HIV/AIDS	Virus	33 million	1.8 million

Spreading disease

One of the main reasons that TB is so dangerous is that it is highly contagious. One person with the disease can pass it on to others just by coughing on them accidentally. A TB **outbreak** is when the disease is detected in two or more people who have been exposed to someone who has TB. In other words, in an outbreak, there are three or more cases that are linked.

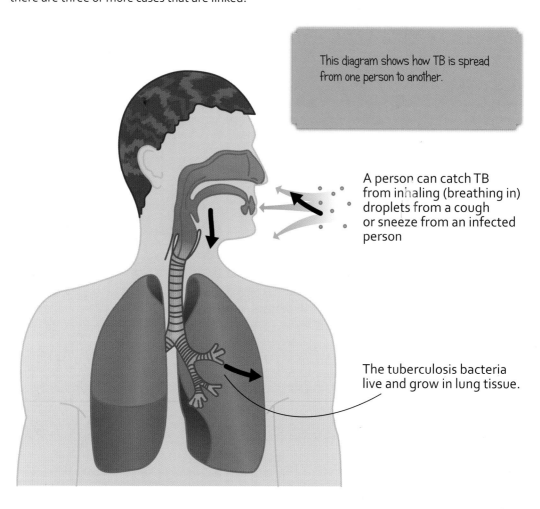

This diagram shows how TB is spread from one person to another.

A person can catch TB from inhaling (breathing in) droplets from a cough or sneeze from an infected person

The tuberculosis bacteria live and grow in lung tissue.

Sometimes it is easy to see the links between TB cases. For example, let's say Jack, the main character in our story, has the disease first, and then other members of his family develop **symptoms**. In this case, it is highly likely that they caught it from him. But often the links are not so obvious, and the investigation becomes trickier. The aim of an investigation is to make sure the disease does not spread any further and endanger the health of more people. Investigations can also lead to recommendations for changes to people's lives that will help prevent the spread of TB in the future.

How an investigation works

Did you know that investigating a possible TB outbreak is like a scientific experiment? Both processes follow logical steps to find and record evidence that supports or rejects an idea, or **hypothesis**:

1. *Hypothesis*: Investigators suggest one or several possible ways that an outbreak could have occurred.
2. *Collecting data*: They search for and carefully record evidence, or **data**, about what actually happened. For example, they may collect medical samples from different people and find out who has been in contact with whom.
3. *Results*: They analyse and discuss the data collected.
4. *Conclusions*: They conclude whether their outbreak hypothesis was correct and recommend steps to take in order to prevent similar outbreaks in the future.

TB AND THE INDUSTRIAL REVOLUTION

In the 19th century, TB may have killed a quarter of the population in Europe. This was partly a result of more people moving to cities to find work in factories during the Industrial Revolution. Many people lived in crowded conditions, where the disease could spread easily.

In the 19th to early 20th centuries, some people with TB were sent to sanatoriums. These were special hospitals where patients had plenty of fresh air, space, good food, and medical care. Many patients felt better after their stays, but the treatment only relieved symptoms and did not tackle the disease.

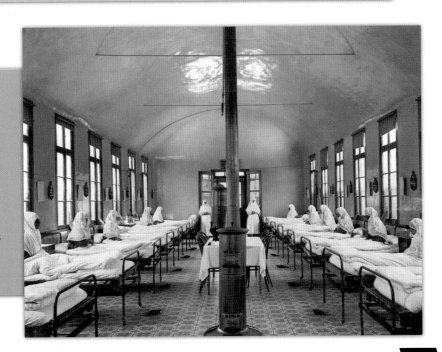

Spotting TB

The first stage of a TB investigation is an examination by a doctor. Jack has had a persistent cough for several weeks and has sometimes coughed up small amounts of blood with the **mucus**. These are symptoms of TB, but also of other illnesses.

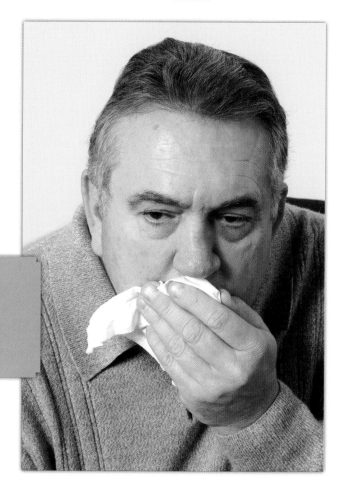

People can cough up blood for a variety of reasons – for example. if they have asthma or pneumonia. which both involve inflammation of the lungs.

During examinations, doctors look for symptoms providing evidence that people are ill. Do any of these also suggest that Jack has TB? Here are some of the things the doctor will check during Jack's examination:

- *Lungs*: Noises made by the lungs while breathing can sound different in people with TB compared to people with healthy lungs. Doctors use a stethoscope to make the sounds easier to hear.

- *Temperature*: People with TB may have a raised temperature that can be checked with a thermometer.

- *Glands*: The doctor checks whether lymph **glands** in the neck or under the arms are swollen, which could indicate an infection somewhere in the body. Sometimes TB can infect other parts of the body, such as the kidneys, bones, or brain.

- *History*: The doctor asks the patient lots of questions and records the answers. For example, the doctor asks if the patient has been feeling well, sweating more than usual, feeling feverish, experiencing any chest pain, eating normally, losing or gaining weight, and sleeping normally.

After the examination, the doctor makes a **diagnosis**. This is the discovery or identification of the cause of illness, based on the evidence the doctor has collected and his or her expert medical knowledge. For Jack, the symptoms suggest either TB or **pneumonia**, but the doctor is not sure which.

Doctors use a stethoscope to listen for crackling sounds. These are caused by damaged airways in the lungs popping open and shut as air moves through them. One cause of this damage is TB.

TB or pneumonia?

This list of symptoms can be associated with TB, pneumonia, or both diseases.

Symtom	TB	Pneumonia
Cough with mucus	✓	✓
Coughing up blood	✓	✓
Poor appetite	✓	✓
Chest pain	✓	✓
Dry cough	✓	✗
Fever	✓	✓
Chills	✗	✓
General weakness	✓	✗
Weight loss	✓	✓
Joint pain	✗	✓

YOU'RE THE INVESTIGATOR!

The doctor thinks pneumonia is a more likely diagnosis than TB for Jack, based on his symptoms. Why should she have asked about any symptoms Jack showed at night? (See the answer on page 14.)

Who investigates?

Doctors are not the only people who investigate a possible TB outbreak. Outbreak investigation is a team effort. That is because an investigation requires people with a variety of specialized skills, plus the investigation may need to happen in many different places at once. An investigation also needs to happen quickly, to prevent the spread of the disease.

Following the trail

All of the investigators use scientific skills and their knowledge of health and disease, which they probably started to learn about in school! But their work can also involve a lot of detective work. The team members may have to follow the trail of TB through a region or even between countries as they work out how TB in one area can spread to another.

Some investigators work for hospitals and clinics or public health departments of local and national governments. They keep records of who has got the disease and link them with records of other cases, using different types of evidence in order to work out the history of the outbreak. This includes places when and times where people may have caught the disease. Some investigators work for special agencies, such as the UK Health Protection Agency, or for charities that work to raise awareness among the public. They may work in partnership with scientists from universities and independent laboratories to carry out tests and to research new ways of treating the disease.

The team members report their different pieces of data and analyses to senior medical experts such as chief medical officers. These people work together to conclude how the outbreak began – and how it can best be stopped.

YOU'RE THE INVESTIGATOR!: THE ANSWER

The doctor later discovered that Jack had been sweating uncontrollably in bed when trying to sleep. **Night sweats** are a common symptom of TB, but they are rarer in people with pneumonia.

Some TB investigators work in well-equipped laboratories set up to rapidly identify TB pathogens. They liaise with other investigators to help stop and prevent outbreaks in groups, communities, and whole populations.

Knowing for certain

The investigation team is still uncertain whether or not Jack has TB. The team members need to know for certain, given the danger of TB. So, they organize a series of tests that could **diagnose** the disease.

Tuberculin test

In a **tuberculin test**, nurses or doctors first clean an area on the underside of the forearm. This removes any bacteria or other pathogens on the skin. They then use a small needle to inject a liquid called tuberculin just under the surface of the skin. Tuberculin is a **protein** made from dead TB bacteria. It is grown in laboratories and will not cause a TB infection.

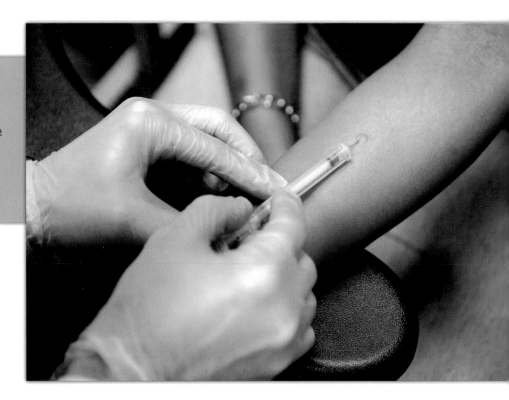

The volume injected in a tuberculin test is tiny and just under the skin, so the immune response happens in one small place.

People who are infected with TB have **white blood cells** that "recognize" the bacteria. So, when these people have a tuberculin test, the white blood cells move in large numbers to the area around the injection site. The white blood cells start to destroy the tuberculin, and this causes an inflamed, raised lump several days later. There is no lump – or it is much smaller – in people who have never been infected before, because their body does not recognize the pathogen.

A white blood cell (coloured pink) flows around and engulfs TB bacteria (coloured yellow). Once it has done this, the white blood cell will chemically destroy these pathogens.

How it works

Your body's **immune system** is a collection of organs, glands, cells, and proteins that work to prevent infectious micro-organisms such as TB from causing disease inside your body. This includes white blood cells called macrophages, which search for and destroy pathogens that have got into the body. Other white blood cells mark intruders for destruction.

Pathogens have chemicals on their surface called **antigens**. When your body detects these antigens, some white blood cells make **antibodies**. These are specialized proteins that can lock onto antigens. White blood cells with antibodies that encounter the right antigen reproduce and make lots of cells that can attack the pathogens rapidly.

In the blood

People can also be tested for TB infection using a blood test. The blood test is quicker than the tuberculin test, but it is more expensive to perform in special laboratory facilities. In the blood test, TB antigens are added to blood. They measure the strength of the immune response, based on the amount of chemical produced by white blood cells. A strong response suggests there is TB in a person's body.

Reading the lump

The lump on Jack's arm after the tuberculin test grows fast. It reaches 25 millimetres (1 inch) across after 36 hours. Usually, health-care workers allow up to 72 hours for a tuberculin test to reach its largest size. But as soon as any tuberculin lump reaches 15 millimetres (2/3 inch) or more, then this is proof that the person injected is infected with TB bacteria.

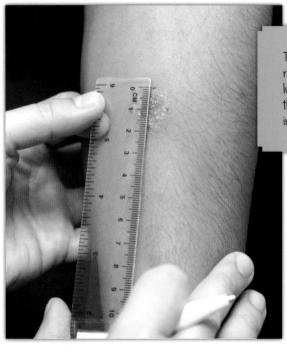

To get the result of the tuberculin test, nurses measure the diameter of the lump across the arm. They include only the actual raised lump and not the red, inflamed area of skin around it.

A smaller lump can still mean someone is infected. How is this true? Well, this is the case for people who have weak immune systems and so produce fewer white blood cells in response to infection. People with weak immune systems include very young children whose immune systems are still developing and those who have had a transplant operation. Small lumps are also taken as positive for TB infection in people known to have been in contact with people who have TB disease, for example.

This diagram illustrates the different possible outcomes after a few days or weeks and after several years, when someone is exposed to TB bacteria.

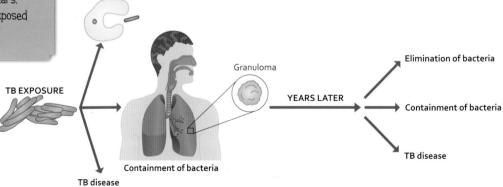

Elimination of bacteria

TB EXPOSURE

Granuloma

YEARS LATER

Elimination of bacteria

Containment of bacteria

TB disease

Containment of bacteria

TB disease

Infection or disease?

Investigators now know that Jack was infected, and his symptoms make it highly likely he has the disease. But being infected does not necessarily mean someone has TB disease. TB bacteria can live in an infected person's lungs for years – or a whole lifetime – without causing any harm. They live inside tiny balls of fibrous tissue called **granulomas** that are made from white blood cells. The bacteria are contained within these balls of cells, preventing them from spreading further.

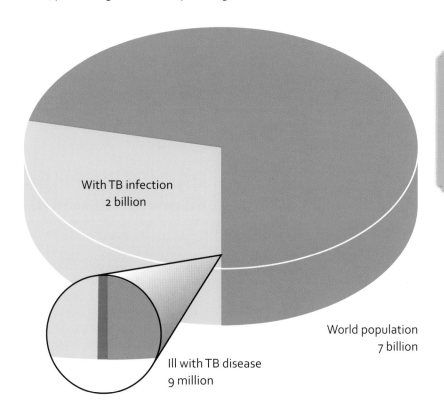

With TB infection
2 billion

World population
7 billion

Ill with TB disease
9 million

Around one-sixth of people sick with TB disease die each year, mostly in countries with poor health care.

In infected people, bacterial numbers are kept down by their immune system. When people have the disease, the amount of TB bacteria grows and their immune system cannot cope. The granulomas can burst open, and the bacteria can spread through the lungs and to other parts of the body. People then get sicker and suffer from TB symptoms.

People who are infected but do not have the disease cannot spread TB. People need to have the disease to be infectious. But infection can turn into disease for different reasons – for example, in people who are ill and so have weak immune systems, have inadequate food, smoke, or suffer from high stress. Infected people have a 1 in 10 chance of developing the disease.

Chest images

The doctors investigating Jack decide to check whether his lungs are showing any signs of having TB disease. In some areas of lungs, bacteria kill lung cells, leaving damaged tissue and cavities that can fill with fluid. In others, lung tissue forms dense lumps of fibrous tissue called nodules around the granulomas, in an attempt to slow the infection.

Doctors can spot tissue damage caused by TB by taking chest images using **X-rays**. Normal lung X-ray images, or **radiographs**, are uniformly grey. But the nodules and fluid-filled cavities on the lungs of people with TB appear lighter than the surrounding lung tissue in radiographs.

However, Jack's radiograph is not conclusive. Radiographers look long and hard at the image, but they are uncertain whether some strange light areas are a sign of TB or the result of a flaw with the machine used to process the images.

HOW X-RAYS WORK

X-rays are a type of energy that moves in rays, similar to the way light travels. Unlike light, X-rays can pass through most solid objects. But different substances absorb the rays by different amounts. For example, hard tissues such as bone absorb more than soft tissues such as air-filled lungs. Bones show up on the film in white areas because few X-rays have got through, but lungs appear darker because more X-rays have got through to form the radiograph.

RADIOGRAPHER

Radiographers take images of patients that can aid in diagnosis and in tracking treatment.

The work of a radiographer involves not only taking X-rays of particular body parts, but also using other ways to take images. These include ultrasound, which uses high-frequency sound, and MRI, which uses magnetism. Radiographers often have a degree in radiography, although some may have trained as doctors first.

YOU'RE THE INVESTIGATOR!

A new radiography assistant forgot to ask Jack to take off his shirt before taking the radiograph. The shirt had unusual metal buttons. Why could this affect the radiograph? (See the answer on page 22.)

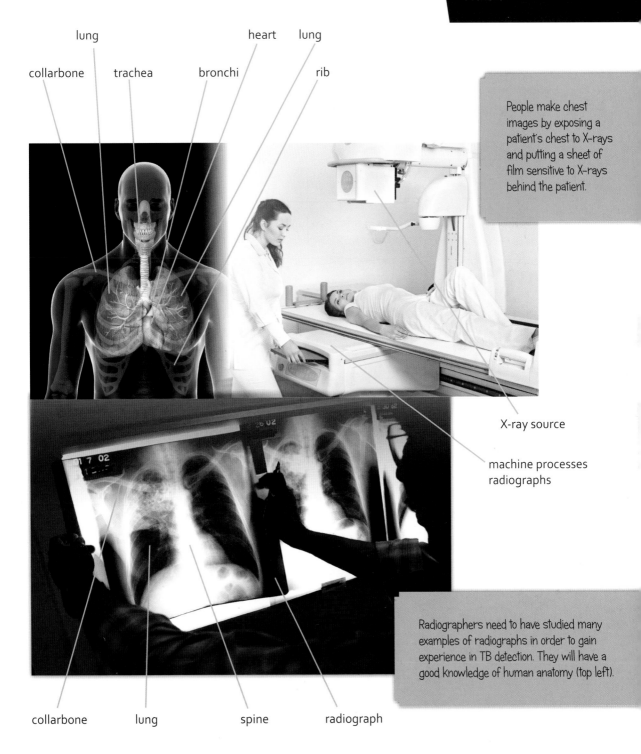

lung   heart   lung

collarbone   trachea   bronchi   rib

People make chest images by exposing a patient's chest to X-rays and putting a sheet of film sensitive to X-rays behind the patient.

X-ray source

machine processes radiographs

collarbone   lung   spine   radiograph

Radiographers need to have studied many examples of radiographs in order to gain experience in TB detection. They will have a good knowledge of human anatomy (top left).

Examining bacteria

Health-care investigators have a positive tuberculin test, but they also have an inconclusive chest X-ray for Jack. So, they need an additional piece of evidence to confirm whether he has the disease or not. This can be achieved by looking closely at **sputum**. This is mucus from the lungs. In people with TB disease, the sputum traps TB bacteria.

Look away now if you are squeamish! A nurse gets Jack to cough up some sputum samples. The sputum samples are taken to a laboratory. Here, technicians begin the next part of the investigation. They smear some sputum on a slide and add chemicals to stain the bacteria present. This takes minutes. Looking under a microscope, they confirm that the bacteria in Jack's sputum resemble TB bacteria. He almost certainly has the disease.

Double-checking

The clearest way to check that the bacteria are definitely TB is to make a **culture**. Technicians put some sputum onto a special type of jelly in a shallow bowl called a petri dish. The jelly supplies nutrients and moisture on which the bacteria grow and reproduce (increase in numbers).

The trouble is that many other sorts of bacteria in the air or on surfaces – not just TB – also grow in the dishes. So, technicians make sure only TB bacteria are present by heating the spoons they use to transfer the sputum. This kills any other types of bacteria on them. They keep the cultures in enclosed containers where air cannot blow new bacteria onto the dishes. The result will finally come through after three weeks. The characteristic pattern

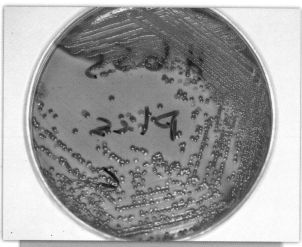

The lines of what look like bubbles on this petri dish are where sputum containing TB bacteria has been put on the jelly. The bubbles are actually lumps of the bacteria growing as they feed on the jelly.

of growth will show that TB bacteria are in Jack's sputum. Other bacteria grow in different patterns. This will be proof that Jack definitely has TB disease.

This view inside lungs. taken by a special instrument called an endoscope. shows the air-filled chambers inside. where TB bacteria can live.

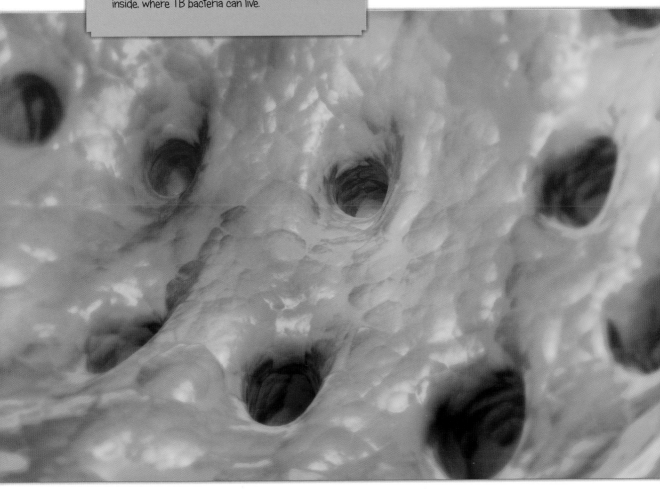

Germ habitat

Why do TB bacteria usually live in the lungs? Because the lungs provide them with an ideal habitat. A living thing's habitat supplies the food, space, and water it needs to live, grow, and reproduce. TB bacteria thrive in the moist, warm, air-filled spaces of the lungs. Compared to other bacteria, TB bacteria reproduce rather slowly. However, each TB cell can split into two cells every 15 to 20 hours in the right conditions.

Who gave it to whom?

The next part in the investigation is to find out which people Jack had been spending time with. These are called his **contacts**. They include contacts who were infected or who developed TB disease after being exposed to him, as well as those who may have given him the disease.

How TB spreads

Tuberculosis bacteria live in the lungs as well as in the throat. They can only move from an infected to an uninfected person through the air. You cannot catch TB from touching infected surfaces. Normal breathing is less likely to spread the bacteria than coughing, sneezing, speaking, or singing. In those instances, there are faster, stronger movements of air that can carry the bacteria greater distances from the lungs in droplets of moisture.

The bacteria are so light that they can remain suspended in the air for several hours and can easily be breathed in by people. How well the disease is transmitted (passed on) to others depends on several things.

A sneeze or cough does not look like much in normal light. But here we can see how a sneeze quickly ejects tiny droplets of mucus and saliva into the air. Someone with TB may also eject tinier droplets containing TB bacteria that other people can easily breathe in.

- *Crowds*: A person with TB may spread the disease to more people if they share the same close space. When other people are further away, they are less likely to breathe in the harmful bacteria.
- *Time*: The longer someone is in contact with a TB sufferer, the more likely it is that that person will catch the disease.
- *Atmospheric conditions*: People are less likely to breathe in TB bacteria when they are in well-ventilated or windy conditions. The air movement spreads out the pathogens. When there is little or no **ventilation**, the bacteria stay in the air.

Jack went from home to school each day by taking a busy tube train. Could this be how he caught the disease? Could he have infected any fellow travellers?

TB HOT SPOTS

Certain conditions make it much more likely for TB to spread.

Risk	Conditions	Examples of places
High	Close quarters for long periods	In the same household, college dormitories, barracks, homeless shelters, offices, nursing homes, and prisons
Intermediate	Close quarters for shorter periods	School classrooms
Lower	Occasional close quarters	Sitting next to people on a bus, tube, or aeroplane; in choir, music, or sport clubs

Contact investigation

Public health workers investigate Jack's contacts. They start by interviewing people he spent hours with each day at home and at school. They ask about which people he had been in contact with, and when and where this had happened. For example, were there any regular visitors to the house? Who were the pupils and teachers Jack spent the most time with at school?

Public health workers need to be patient and thorough when interviewing people during a TB outbreak investigation. Then they have a better chance of helping to identify contacts and restrict the spread of the disease.

Contact investigators need good detective skills, because people cannot always remember things accurately. For example, investigators spot some toys in Jack's house and find after asking that they do not belong to any family members. Jack's parents then remember that another child had come to the house many times to play with Jack's siblings a few months before.

Investigators also spot a photo of Jack's aunt with the family taken 18 months before. Jack's mum mentions how her sister – Jack's aunt – had been visiting from Jamaica, where she lives. She recalls how Jack had spent lots of time with his aunt, and that the aunt had been feeling a little unwell during her stay.

They then investigate people he had spent less time with, such as people at the gym Jack went to once a week and commuters on the tube. This is much trickier, because Jack does not know the people. So, for example, they watch tube videos of travellers Jack had sat near. They then identify and interview these travellers when they are next spotted at the station.

Test the contacts

Investigators draw up a list of contacts. They refer them to health centres for TB testing and also examine public health records. This is so they can see if doctors had discovered TB infections or treated TB disease in any of the people, or their families, in the past. They discover the following:

- *With TB disease*: Jack's sister, his best friend from school, a temporary music teacher who has left the school, and one commuter
- *With TB infection*: Jack's brother, 11 pupils from his class, seven commuters
- *Treated for TB in the past*: One commuter, a gym worker, Jack's aunt who lives in Jamaica.

DayS 4-5: Jack's contacts are tested; investigators identify other contacts.

DayS 5-6: Experts interview and test more distant contacts.

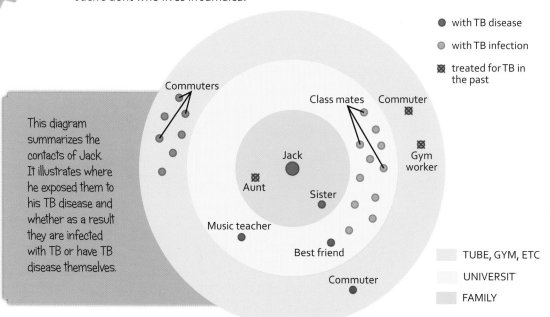

This diagram summarizes the contacts of Jack. It illustrates where he exposed them to his TB disease and whether as a result they are infected with TB or have TB disease themselves.

- with TB disease
- with TB infection
- treated for TB in the past

TUBE, GYM, ETC

UNIVERSIT

FAMILY

Commuters · Class mates · Commuter · Jack · Gym worker · Aunt · Sister · Music teacher · Best friend · Commuter

From diagnosis to treatment

People investigating a TB outbreak do not waste any time, because they have to make sure they prevent the spread of the disease. Here are some typical periods in an investigation once a contact is identified. He or she is:

- interviewed within three days
- TB tested within five days
- started on treatment (if TB positive) after 10 days.

The same source?

There are lots of people in the world with TB, so how do investigators find out who might have infected Jack? To answer this question, investigators can find out more about the TB bacteria.

All TB bacterial cells look very similar and grow nearly identical cultures in a laboratory. But, in fact, there are different **strains**, or types, of TB. Worldwide, there are around 12,000 different strains! So, if Jack has one strain of TB and one of his contacts has exactly the same strain, then this means one person probably infected the other. Scientists can distinguish strains by looking at **chromosomes** inside TB bacterial cells.

DNA differences

Chromosomes are made of spirals of protein called DNA. Each chromosome contains thousands of different genes. We can think of genes as a living thing's instruction manual. A gene contains sequences of DNA with a distinct pattern of chemicals, forming a code. This code provides essential instructions about everything from how the living thing will look to the way its body functions.

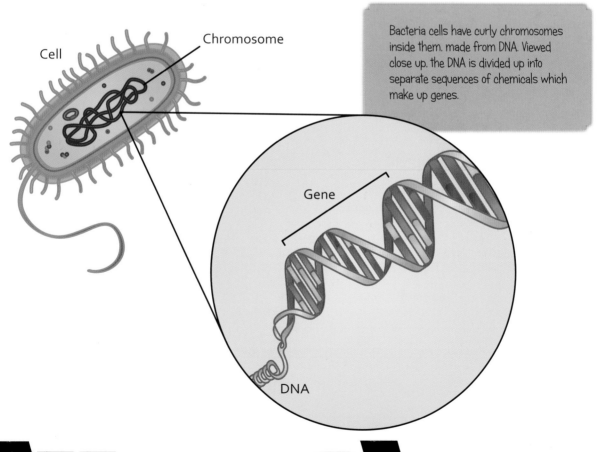

Cell

Chromosome

Gene

DNA

Bacteria cells have curly chromosomes inside them. made from DNA. Viewed close up. the DNA is divided up into separate sequences of chemicals which make up genes.

All TB cells have nearly identical genes. However, in between the important stretches of code are pieces of less important DNA that differ greatly among individuals. The process of **genotyping**, or DNA fingerprinting, uses scientific tests to reveal those differences.

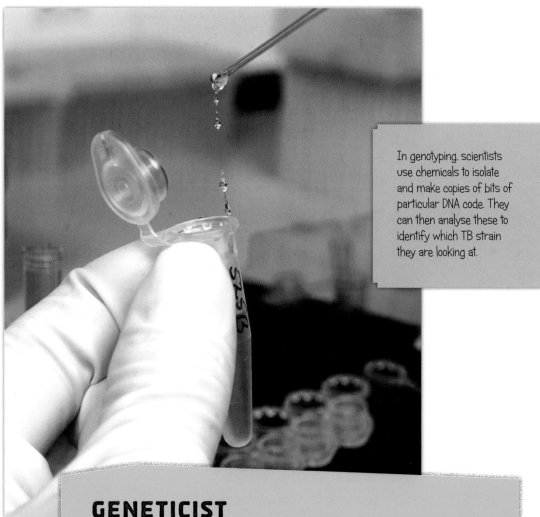

In genotyping, scientists use chemicals to isolate and make copies of bits of particular DNA code. They can then analyse these to identify which TB strain they are looking at.

GENETICIST

Geneticists study genes, DNA, and chromosomes.

There are many types of geneticists. Some carry out the genotyping for pathogens such as TB, in addition to testing samples from crime scenes that might help police identify victims or criminals. Others help to create genetically modified organisms such as crops resistant to disease. All geneticists will usually have studied biology and often chemistry at university.

How genotyping works

Genotyping is carried out by highly trained laboratory workers, using a variety of equipment. It is quite complicated. But the basic method is as follows:

1. Take a sample of TB bacteria from a culture made with sputum from one person with TB.
2. Add special substances called enzymes. These recognize the bits of DNA that usually differ between individuals and detach them from the rest. The fragments are of different lengths because they have different numbers of repeating sequences of chemicals.
3. Put the mixture of different-length fragments onto a sheet of gel in a salt solution. An electric current is passed through the gel. This makes the fragments move across it.

   Bigger fragments do not travel as far through the gel as smaller fragments. The different-sized fragments collect at different levels, or bands, through the gel. The width of a band depends on the amount of the particular fragment.
4. Add more chemicals, to make the pattern of bands more visible.
5. Repeat the procedure for samples from other people with TB. Compare their band patterns to see how closely they match.

This is a banding pattern from genotyping TB samples from different people. Scientists look for matching patterns between different samples that can confirm whether the people have the same strain of TB and are therefore likely to be part of the same TB outbreak.

Matching genotypes

For Jack's case, genotyping produces some interesting results. The banding pattern of Jack's TB bacterial samples matches those of his sister and his best friend, but not those of the music teacher and commuter who had the disease. Geneticists had assumed that the patients had the same strain of TB, forming a genotype **cluster**. Since Jack developed TB symptoms first, it is very likely he gave the disease to his sister and best friend.

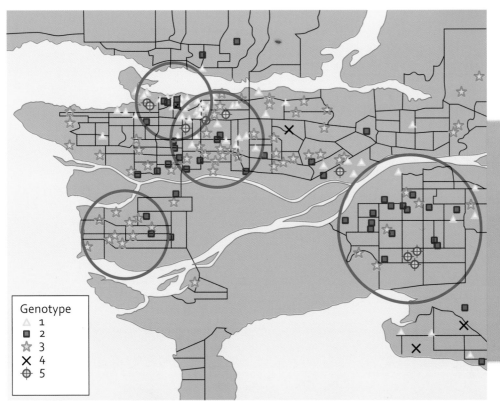

This map of Vancouver shows symbols for contacts infected by one of five different genotypes of TB. Geneticists use maps such as this to help identify genotype clusters (the four large red circles) and see how TB cases might be linked.

Genotype
△ 1
◼ 2
☆ 3
✕ 4
⊕ 5

Day 21: Genotyping results show that Jack's strain matches those of his sister and best friend.

Day 24: Genotyping results show that the music teacher and commuter have a different strain of the disease.

YOU'RE THE INVESTIGATOR!

Genotype databases show that Jack's TB strain is a rare one from Jamaica, a place he has never visited. What is the contact link between Jack and Jamaica, and can you explain why he might have this strain? (See the answer on page 32.)

Preventing the spread of TB

The investigation team members know several things about Jack. He has an unusual strain of TB and is at the centre of a TB outbreak. The team members have to act urgently to prevent the outbreak from getting out of control. Preventing the spread of TB requires three steps:

1. Use drugs to kill the TB bacteria.
2. Keep TB sufferers away from others they might infect while they have the disease.
3. Improve ventilation or other aspects of the places where people live or spend time, to make it less likely that they will become infected by future TB outbreaks.

Drug treatment

Nurses immediately start to treat Jack, his sister, and his best friend with **antibiotics**. These are drugs that can be used inside the body to treat bacterial infections such as TB. They work by disrupting essential life processes in bacteria – for example, they stop them from getting energy from food or reproducing. The patients are surprised to hear that the treatment will take six months. Contacts with TB infection are also treated, but with a shorter course of fewer antibiotics. A nurse tells Jack that his treatment for TB in the lungs is half the length of time needed to treat TB in other parts of the body.

Keep taking the medicine

You have probably been warned to always finish a course of antibiotics, or else they will not work. Some individual bacteria survive antibiotic treatment better than others, and these can thrive and reproduce, forming separate strains when the amount of antibiotic used against them is insufficient. This can happen, for example, when people take too few tablets, take them too infrequently, or stop taking the tablets because they are feeling better. Antibiotics can no longer affect these strains of bacteria.

This is an example of **drug resistance**. TB drug resistance worldwide is a major problem, because people do not always take the antibiotics properly, and strains are emerging that cannot easily be treated with conventional, cheaper medicines.

YOU'RE THE INVESTIGATOR!: THE ANSWER

Jack probably became infected with TB by his aunt from Jamaica when she visited. Although he has not seen her for 18 months, the infection eventually turned into the disease.

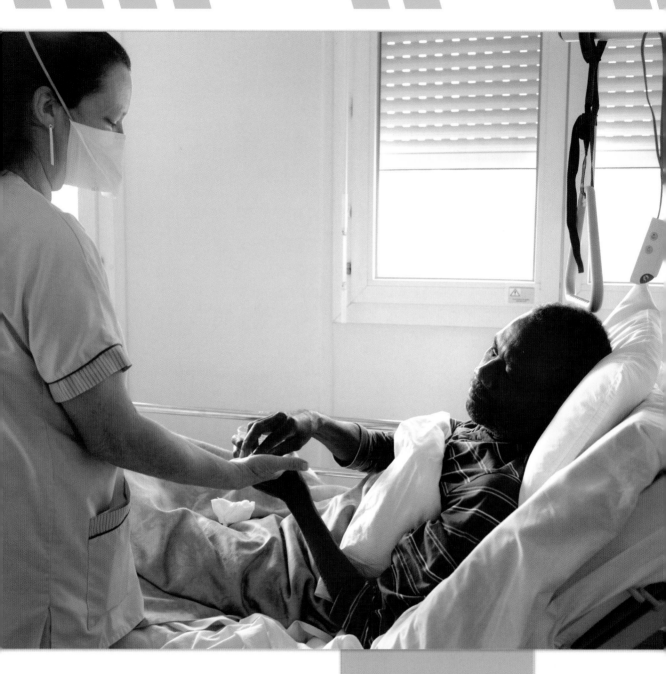

When nurses and other caseworkers monitor the dose and frequency of drugs that a TB patient takes, it reduces the emergence and spread of drug-resistant strains.

Treatment problems

After one week, treatment is going well for Jack. New **sputum smears** of Jack, his sister, and his friend reveal fewer bacteria, and their lung radiographs are clearer. But then some new dark patches appear on their radiographs. The patients' symptoms worsen – Jack's friend has particularly bad night sweats. By now, the parents of the children are getting very worried.

Doctors realize that the antibiotics are not working because the TB strain is drug resistant. They call doctors treating Jack's other contacts with TB disease. These patients are also not responding to treatment, and the doctors agree to try a different combination of antibiotics. This means even more tablets and also injections. Thankfully, these work! By one month after the start of treatment, they all start to get better. Repeat sputum smears show few TB bacteria, and radiographs are clear.

Everyone is very relieved that this TB strain is not **multidrug-resistant TB (MDR-TB)**. If it had been, the patients may have had to take antibiotics for two years. The cost of treating MDR-TB is also much higher than normal TB, as the table shows:

The cost of treating MDR-TB in India		
	TB	**MDR-TB**
Cost per patient to treat	$20	$2,000–$12,000
Tablets per day	2–4	14 + injection
Length of treatment	6 months	2 years

MICROBIOLOGIST

Microbiologists study the natural history and variation in micro-organisms such as TB.

A microbiologist may identify strains of pathogens, find new ways of detecting infection, or help develop new antibiotics to treat drug-resistant strains of TB. Most microbiologists have degrees in biomedical science or biology (even microbiology!) and may work in laboratories in industries, hospitals, or universities.

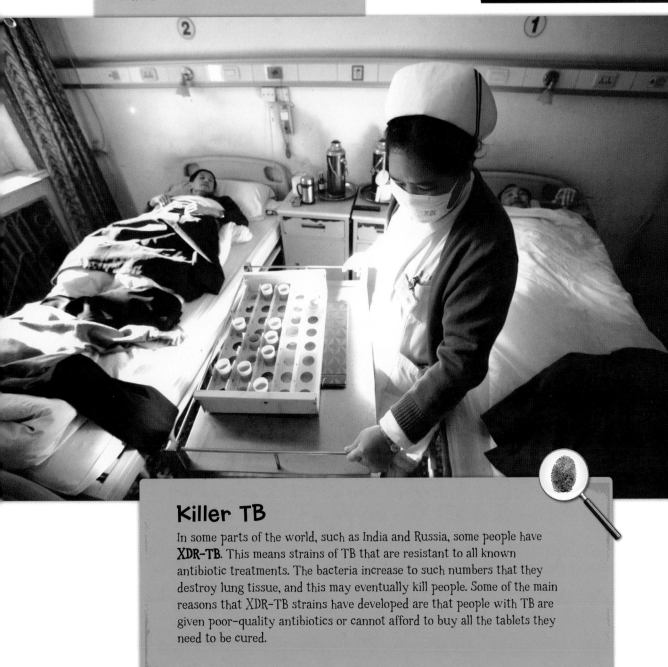

A nurse gives a combination of medicines to patients with MDR-TB at the Beijing Chest Hospital in China.

Day 21: Doctors change the antibiotics used for Jack, his sister, and his best friend.

Killer TB

In some parts of the world, such as India and Russia, some people have **XDR-TB**. This means strains of TB that are resistant to all known antibiotic treatments. The bacteria increase to such numbers that they destroy lung tissue, and this may eventually kill people. Some of the main reasons that XDR-TB strains have developed are that people with TB are given poor-quality antibiotics or cannot afford to buy all the tablets they need to be cured.

Isolation

The patients stay in the hospital for the first four weeks of treatment. This is to isolate them from other family members, pupils and workers from the school, and other possible contacts. This also helps doctors to collect and test sputum regularly, observe the patients for any symptoms that need treatment, and ensure that the patients take their medicine at exactly the right intervals. So, how do the nurses and doctors treating the TB patients avoid breathing in TB bacteria?

Jack, his sister, and his best friend are each kept in **respiratory isolation**. This means they are each kept in a private, sealed room where the bacteria they breathe out are not a risk to others in the hospital. Clean air is constantly pumped into the room, and all air leaving the room passes through a special filter to remove TB bacteria. Their nurses, doctors, and any visitors always wear disposable air filter masks while in the rooms. After about four weeks, the patients are allowed to go home.

At home, Jack's parents work closely with visiting nurses to manage his and his sister's treatment. Visitors are kept to a minimum, and the patients are not allowed back at school or in other public spaces for three months. Luckily, most of this time is during the summer holiday, so they do not miss many classes. And Jack will get to take his exams the following term. He will even give a presentation to his class about the dangers of TB, because he knows so much about it!

FEATURES OF AN ISOLATION ROOM

Isolation rooms often have the following features:

- *Changing air.* Patients should not re-breathe in TB bacteria they have breathed out. Therefore, the air in the room is changed at least 12 times per hour.

- *Lower air pressure inside than outside*: When a gas is at high pressure, lots of its **molecules** are packed into a space. Gases move from high to low pressure areas, because there is more room for the molecules to fill. This means that when the isolation room door opens, air flows in, so bacteria are less likely to get out.

- *HEPA filters*: TB bacteria have a minimum width of 0.5 microns. (A micron is one millionth of a metre; 1 metre equals 3.3 feet.) HEPA filters have holes that are even smaller than this. The filters remove 99.97 per cent of particles larger than 0.3 microns wide.

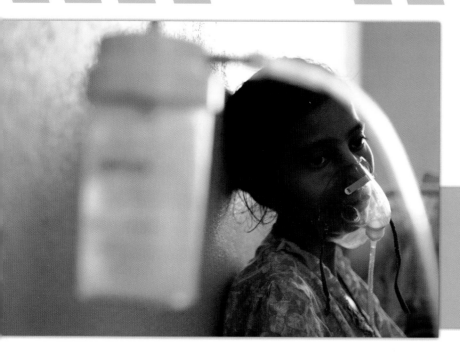

Day 8: The three pupils are started on antibiotics in isolation in the hospital.

Day 35: Jack, his sister, and his friend are well enough to go home.

In isolation, patients who are infectious breathe into a respirator. This filters out TB bacteria to prevent them from going into air that other people might breathe in.

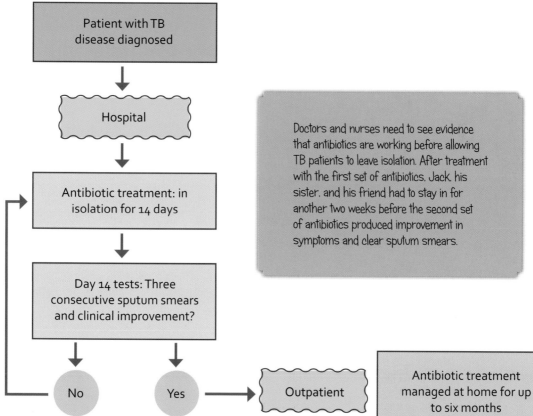

Patient with TB disease diagnosed

↓

Hospital

↓

Antibiotic treatment: in isolation for 14 days

↓

Day 14 tests: Three consecutive sputum smears and clinical improvement?

↓   ↓

No   Yes → Outpatient → Antibiotic treatment managed at home for up to six months

Doctors and nurses need to see evidence that antibiotics are working before allowing TB patients to leave isolation. After treatment with the first set of antibiotics, Jack, his sister, and his friend had to stay in for another two weeks before the second set of antibiotics produced improvement in symptoms and clear sputum smears.

Controlling movement

While Jack is at home recovering, he sees a news report on television. His music teacher who had TB disease has been arrested at the airport! The man had been feeling so much better while in respiratory isolation that he walked out of the hospital. Doctors at the hospital got his culture results and found that the teacher has MDR-TB.

The TB team at the hospital tried to call the teacher, but he did not reply. They got in touch with the local airport because the teacher had been talking about needing to fly to play at a music festival in Germany. He was checking in for his flight at the airport when an airline agent stopped him from travelling. The teacher was at risk of worsening symptoms because he had not finished his antibiotics. He was also at risk of infecting others with MDR-TB.

More and more people travel by air each year, and there is great potential for the spread of TB infection between countries, not to mention while sitting near other passengers on aeroplanes.

Border controls

Most countries have border control agencies that work closely with airlines and other transport networks to control the movement of people or goods internationally. One of their jobs is to identify people with infectious diseases, such as TB. Any patient with TB who has plans to travel should always talk to his or her doctor and nurses. These experts can then make sure a patient is not an infection risk and has enough medicine to continue treatment while away.

Day 25: The music teacher infected with TB is stopped at the airport.

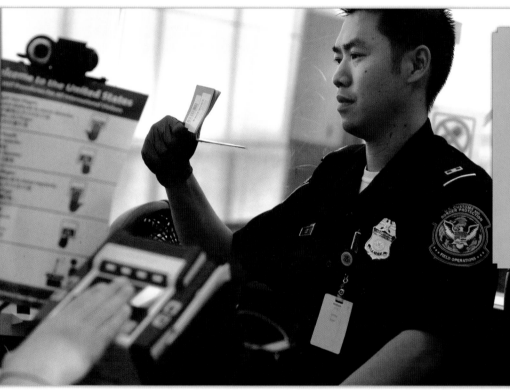

Border patrol officials check fingerprints and papers to identify travellers boarding aeroplanes. Once they have made an identification they may be alerted to health information about the passenger such as TB status that could affect whether they allow the passenger to travel.

Quarantine

In most cases, people with TB are happy to be treated so that they will feel better. But sometimes people do not agree to receive treatment when they are diagnosed – for example, if they want to travel to another place for treatment or if they have religious beliefs that do not allow medical treatment. In such cases, people are sometimes put into quarantine. This is when they are legally forced to be examined, to complete medical treatment in isolation, and to not travel until they can no longer infect others.

Eradicating TB

The investigation team has completed its work in stopping the outbreak. The remaining missing piece in the puzzle is why Jack's aunt had TB in the first place. And what recommendations could they make to help prevent or even **eradicate** (get rid of) TB in the future?

People at risk

Jack's aunt was a charity worker in Jamaica. Her job included helping to improve conditions for prisoners. Worldwide, TB disease is the single biggest cause of death among prisoners. They often live in crowded conditions with poor ventilation. The investigation team concludes that the aunt probably contracted the disease from a prisoner. Maybe Jack's TB infection had turned into the disease because he had another illness that weakened his immune system. The stress of studying for important exams may have tired him out and reduced his resistance to the disease even more.

Anyone can catch TB. But most of the people who become ill are in groups that are at higher risk because of their lifestyle or the environments they live in. These include people who use illegal drugs and people who are very poor or homeless. When people have inadequate food or shelter or use drugs, their immune systems can become weaker. They also often have little money to spend on TB screening and medical care.

In a homeless shelter, people who may usually live in poor conditions with limited health checks can converge and risk exposing each other to TB and other infectious diseases.

Better environments

One way to reduce the risk of TB is to improve environmental conditions. For example, environmental health workers can visit prisons and homeless shelters to assess and make recommendations about reducing overcrowding and improving ventilation. Following the TB outbreak at the school, the investigation team recommends that new fans and better-opening windows be fitted in classrooms. That way, if someone has the disease, any TB bacteria the person coughs or sneezes out into the air will be flushed out of the building more effectively.

Workers fit an improved ventilation system for a space to be used by the public. This will ensure that airflow is speeded up and help flush out any pathogens such as TB bacteria from the space.

HIV and TB

HIV (human immunodeficiency virus) is a pathogen that attacks the body's immune system, making it less able to withstand infections by other pathogens. TB is the most common infection in people with HIV. It also accelerates the progression of HIV to AIDS (acquired immunodeficiency syndrome). AIDS is the final stage in HIV infection, when a person's immune system can no longer fight life-threatening infections. Around one-third of people with HIV/AIDS die of TB.

Better treatment

Jack is lucky to live where he does. He had access to excellent health care to manage his TB. But people in many countries and other situations are not so lucky. His aunt told him that one of the biggest problems affecting TB in prisons was transfers. If a prisoner being treated for TB was transferred to another prison, then the prisoner's treatment was not always continued. When this happens, prisoners are more likely to help produce drug-resistant TB strains.

One of the main ways to improve treatment is by **DOT**, which means "directly observed therapy". Nurses or other people responsible for treatment watch people as they take their medicines and keep detailed records of their treatment. Another way is to spot TB infection by carrying out more tuberculin tests on people and providing X-ray and laboratory services to confirm the disease more rapidly. But both DOT and TB testing can be expensive, and some developing countries cannot or do not spend enough money to provide adequate health care to all.

Education and training

A major part of eradicating TB is education. Following the outbreak, the school Jack attends organizes presentations both for pupils and their parents. These have information about the signs of TB disease, what treatment involves, and how important it is to report possible cases to stop outbreaks. Health-care workers also need up-to-date training about new strains of TB and how best to tackle them.

EPIDEMIOLOGIST

Epidemiologists study the frequency and distribution of diseases within human populations and environments.

Epidemiologists interview the public and examine health records to find data about who has a disease. They examine how factors such as travel, culture, living conditions, age, and health affect the spread of disease, and how changes in the way people live can prevent disease. Epidemiologists usually have a degree in biology or chemistry and additional specialized qualifications in public health.

Women and children in Ghana attend a clinic with a poster informing the public about TB risks. Effective. engaging public education programmes can help to slow the spread of TB worldwide.

Inject to protect

Many countries worldwide have TB **vaccination** programmes to help protect people against the disease. This is when a particular section of the population is injected with a vaccine containing TB bacteria. The TB vaccine is called **BCG**, which stands for "Bacille Calmette-Guérin" and is named after two French scientists. BCG is made up of a weakened form of TB found in cattle. After someone is vaccinated, the body makes antibodies to the pathogen that is very similar to human TB. Then, if vaccinated people are exposed to TB in the future, their immune systems recognize the pathogens and destroy them.

Governments with TB vaccination programmes usually advise that BCG is given to babies in their first few months of life. This is when they are least likely to have been exposed to TB bacteria. Early protection is considered important, because if children develop TB disease in their lungs, it can spread more easily to the brain or other organs than in adults. But BCG vaccinations are generally less effective after people reach adulthood. Also, people who have been given BCG may give a positive tuberculin test, even though they are not infected with TB.

Some governments, such as the United Kingdom, vaccinate only people at high risk of catching TB, such as babies born in areas with high rates of TB or adults working with TB patients in hospitals or in prisons. Other governments, such as in the United States, prefer to fund TB screening and networks of TB nurses to manage TB treatment, rather than expensive vaccination programmes.

In our story, investigators find that Jack's aunt had missed an appointment for a TB vaccination before working in the prison. This may have contributed to her becoming infected.

STOP TB

STOP TB is a global TB eradication programme coordinated by the World Health Organization (WHO), which represents most countries in the world. It promotes the use of TB vaccines and DOT strategies to combat the disease. This involves working with charities and pharmaceutical companies to develop better vaccines and cheaper TB antibiotics, and also funding TB health care in poorer countries.

Worldwide TB vaccination rates

North America

Europe

Asia

Africa

Australasia

South America

percentage of people vaccinated

50   80   90%

This world map shows where BCG vaccination against TB is highest. Did you have a BCG vaccination when you were younger?

Keeping TB in check

This story of a TB outbreak shows how a team of TB investigators can work together to safeguard public health. It involves collecting, analysing, and making conclusions from data about the infection and disease, and about a patient's movements and contacts. It involves making conclusions about who gave the infection to whom, and how to make changes to make a future outbreak less likely. Here is a summary of the stages in the investigation:

Medical examination: Symptoms suggest TB

↓

Tuberculin test: Size of lump confirms infection

↓

X-ray: Radiograph inconclusive

↓

Sputum smear: Confirms disease

↓

Interview people and check health records: Contacts identified

↓

Antibiotics: Treatment for those with TB disease and TB infection

↓

Genotyping: Check the strain in different contacts and identify the TB cluster

↓

Conclusion: Identify the original source of TB and transmission route

↓

Changes to prevent future outbreaks: Improve the school environment and promote TB education

Coordinated response

Dealing with a TB outbreak is complicated. Like any disease, it is usually easiest to spot once symptoms appear. But by then, someone may have been infecting other people for some time. The process of trying to eradicate TB is also very complicated and requires a coordinated response. It is a balance between preventative measures – such as improving environments and giving out vaccinations to prevent infection – and speedy medical screening and treatment for those already infected or suffering from the disease. Globally, coordinated responses are making a difference. Between 1990 and 2011, deaths caused by TB fell by one-third. The WHO target is to cut the death rate by half.

Tiffany Rodriguez Esquivel nearly died from MDR-TB that she got from her father. Neither he nor Tiffany finished their course of treatment as the family thought they could recover by taking vitamin supplements. Poor education about drug-resistant TB such as this is making the treatment of the disease harder and more expensive around the world.

CHINESE SUCCESS

In 1991, the Chinese government started a TB disease control programme by training health workers to use DOT to treat TB patients at clinics across the country. They kept full records of treatments, which were reported to a National Tuberculosis Project Office. Ten years later, TB cases had fallen by over one-third and 30,000 fewer people died of TB each year, compared to the death rate before making the changes. Successful treatment cost less than $100 per person.

Bill Gates (centre), billionaire owner of Microsoft, meeting Dr Margaret Chan, WHO Director-General at a meeting in 2009 where he pledged money from his charitable foundation to tackling TB in China.

Investigation: the spread of pathogens

TB pathogens spread through the air. Many other pathogens spread from surfaces where they are resting via hands into mouths when we eat, touch our faces, lick our fingers, and so on. The spread of these pathogens can be reduced if people wash their hands properly. But how well do you wash your hands? Here is an activity you can carry out with friends or classmates to measure hand-washing abilities!

Hypothesis: Washing hands in warm water and soap will clean dirt from them more effectively than when using cold water and no soap.

What you will need

- cooking oil
- cinnamon or powdered nutmeg
- a teaspoon
- 4 bars of soap or a pump-action liquid soap dispenser
- two sinks, one containing warm water and one containing cold water
- paper towels
- a stopwatch

What to do

1. Prepare a results table as below. Choose one person to record data on the table. Set up the sinks with water, paper towels, and soap.

Duration of wash			
Hand-washing method	10 seconds	20 seconds	30 seconds
Cold water only	1		
Cold water + soap			
Warm water only			
Warm water + soap			

2. Four people should each coat their hands in cooking oil by getting a small amount and rubbing it around. Then, get a half-teaspoon of cinnamon or nutmeg on each person's hands to rub in. This is used as dirt in the experiment, to simulate pathogens.

3. Each person will use a different hand-washing method: just cold water, cold water with soap, just warm water, or warm water with soap. Everyone should wet their hands with the right temperature water and have soap ready – but no scrubbing!

4. The first experiment is washing hands for 10 seconds. Use the stopwatch to tell people when to start and when to finish.

5. Judge how dirty their hands are after the 10-second wash duration as follows: 1=nasty, 2=half-clean, 3=spotless. Record your results.

6. Now the people with dirty hands should use paper towels to clean their hands. Then repeat steps 2 to 5 for 20-second and 30-second wash durations.

Compare the data in the table showing different washing methods. Which was most effective? Did it match up with your hypothesis? Did washing duration make a difference? Do you think that pathogens stick to hands as well as spices stick to oily hands?

The amount of soap and the vigour of rubbing hands vary among different people. Can you think of any other things that vary among experiments? How do you think all these variables might affect results and conclusions?

THE POWER OF HAND WASHING

Did you know that 80 per cent of common infections are spread by hands? Washing hands often and properly (with soap), especially before you cook, prepare, or eat food and after using the toilet, dramatically decreases the frequency of colds, flu, and other infections. It also saves lives. The two biggest killers of children in many parts of the world with poor access to medical care are diarrhoeal disease and respiratory (nose, throat, and lung) infections.

Timeline

This timeline shows the progress of the investigation of Jack's TB. Real investigations might follow a similar but slightly different timeline.

Time	Events
18 months before	Jack's aunt visits from Jamaica and spends time with him. She had a history of TB in the past.
2 weeks before	The first medical examination concludes that Jack has pneumonia.
Day 1	A doctor examines Jack for a second time as his symptoms worsen. He concludes that Jack might have TB. A nurse carries out a tuberculin test.
Day 3	The tuberculin test comes up positive for TB infection; an X-ray is inconclusive; a sputum sample is taken, and the smear is positive for bacteria resembling TB; a sputum culture is started; Jack is interviewed about possible contacts.
Days 4–5	Jack's family and pupils and teachers from his school are tested for TB infection; investigators identify other, more distant contacts among underground commuters and gym workers; checking health records reveals that the boy's aunt and several other contacts had TB in the past.
Days 6–7	Experts interview and test other, more distant contacts.
Day 8	X-ray and sputum results reveal that Jack's sister and best friend have TB disease, too. The three pupils are started on antibiotics in isolation in the hospital and have sputum samples taken for genotyping.
Day 9	Test results reveal that a former teacher and a commuter also have TB disease, and that an additional 19 contacts have TB infection. They start treatment.

Day 21	Genotyping results show that Jack's strain matches that of his sister and friend and also his aunt. Doctors do not see improvement in the TB patients, so they change the antibiotics used.
Day 22	A sputum culture finally confirms TB disease.
Day 24	Genotyping results show that the music teacher and the commuter have a different strain from Jack, his sister, his friend, and his aunt.
Day 25	The music teacher with TB is stopped from travelling at the airport.
Day 35	The TB patients' symptoms are much improved and Jack, his sister, and his friend have clear sputum smears. They go home for continued, managed treatment by their parents and nurses.
3 months	The pupils return to school.
6 months	Jack, his sister, and his friend have their final antibiotic treatments.
2 years	Jack's former teacher with MDR-TB has his final antibiotic treatment.

Glossary

antibiotic substance that can prevent growth or destroy bacteria to slow or end infections

antibody substance made by the immune system to fight pathogens

antigen substance that enters a living thing and can cause a disease

bacterium (plural: **bacteria**) tiny, simple organism that lives in all environments. Some bacteria can be helpful but others are harmful to living things.

BCG short for "Bacille Calmette-Guérin", it is a type of vaccine used to help prevent TB

chromosome thread-shaped structure in cells that carries genes

cluster group of things of the same type, such as people with identical strains of TB, that appear near to each other

contact person who may be infected, and may possibly infect others, because he or she has been in contact with someone with an infectious disease

culture growth of cells or bacteria, usually in a laboratory for medical or scientific study

data information, facts, or numbers collected for use or analysis

developing country country with low income and poor standards in health, nutrition, education, and industry

diagnose discover or identify the cause of an illness or problem

diagnosis discovery or identification of the cause of an illness or problem by an expert such as a doctor

DOT short for "directly observed therapy", it is a system of checking to make sure that people take their medicine, especially antibiotics that if not taken can lead to drug resistance

drug resistance when drugs do not work because pathogens are no longer affected by them. This is usually caused by other people not completing courses of drugs or taking inadequate amounts, so pathogens get used to them.

eradicate wipe out or end totally

genotyping working out the differences and similarities between genes in different individuals or types of organism

gland organ in a living thing that produces a useful substance. For example, glands in the mouth produce saliva, which helps us swallow food.

granuloma hard growth of cells in tissue. For example, TB cells in the lungs of an infected person may be found in a granuloma.

hypothesis idea or explanation for something that awaits proof using scientific observation, recording data, and conclusions based on that data

immune system organs, cells, and tissues that work together to protect a living thing from disease caused mostly by pathogens

infection when pathogens not normally present invade and increase in numbers in body tissues, often causing harm

infectious disease disease such as TB caused by pathogen infection

microorganism type of tiny living thing, such as bacteria, that cannot easily be seen without a microscope

molecule two or more atoms

mucus slimy substance made by tissues and glands to protect the body. For example, mucus in our nose and throat help to trap dust and bacteria.

multidrug-resistant TB (MDR-TB) one of several strains of TB that cannot be treated with the normal group of drugs and requires special, more expensive treatment

night sweats bouts of heavy sweating that occur at night

outbreak larger than normal occurrence of cases of disease in a particular area, season, or community

pathogen living thing that causes a disease

pneumonia inflammation of the lungs usually caused by pathogens

protein type of chemical substance in all cells, each with different roles in making living things function properly

radiograph image produced using X-rays

respiratory isolation keeping someone in conditions where he or she cannot breathe out pathogens onto other people or breathe in pathogens from other people

sputum mucus from the throat or lungs that is generally coughed up. The cells or pathogens caught in sputum can be used in the diagnosis of some diseases.

sputum smear when sputum is grown in controlled conditions on special jelly to increase the numbers of pathogens, to help in their identification

strain particular variety of a type of organism, often a pathogen

symptom change in an organism that shows that it is unhealthy

tissue group of similar cells that together carry out a role for an organism. For example, bone is a tough tissue that is important for supporting the body in many animals.

tuberculin test skin test to help identify a past or present infection by TB bacteria

tuberculosis (TB) infectious and sometimes fatal disease caused by *Mycobacterium tuberculosis* growth in tissues, especially the lungs

vaccination give people or animals a substance into their blood that protects them from disease. A vaccine is often made from a safe form of a pathogen.

ventilation improve the flow of fresh air into a space

virus tiny cell that is only active once inside another cell and that causes infectious disease

white blood cell special type of cell in blood that helps the body get rid of pathogens

XDR-TB one of several strains of TB that cannot be treated with any drugs

X-ray type of ray that can pass through objects that are not transparent and can be used to create internal images

Find out more

Books

Cells and Disease (Investigating Cells), Barbara A. Somervill (Heinemann Library, 2011)

Health and Disease (Headline Issues), Sarah Levete (Heinemann Library, 2009)

Fighting Infectious Diseases (Microlife), Robert Snedden (Heinemann Library, 2008)

Fighting Infectious Diseases (Science at the Edge), Sally Morgan (Heinemann Library, 2009)

Infectious Diseases (Mapping Global Issues), Anne Rooney (Franklin Watts, 2011)

Pox, Pus & Plague: A History of Disease and Infection (Painful History of Medicine), John Townsend (Raintree, 2006)

Websites

www.hpa.org.uk/Topics/InfectiousDiseases/InfectionsAZ
Visit the Health Protection Agency's website to find an A-Z of infectious diseases such as TB, influenza, and AIDS.

www.medicalcareers.nhs.uk/considering_medicine/introduction.aspx
Have you ever considered a career in medicine, such as becoming a doctor or nurse? Visit these web pages to learn more.

outbreaks.globalincidentmap.com/home.php
This map shows where disease outbreaks are happening in the world right now.

www.tbalert.org/general/faq.php
This web site answers some frequently asked questions about TB.

www.tbalert.org/news_press/TBHistoricalTimeline.htm
See a timeline of tuberculosis outbreaks, medical breakthroughs, and attempts to halt the disease.

webadventures.rice.edu/stu/Games/MedMyst
Try investigating infectious disease outbreaks by taking part in the online games at this site.

www.who.int/csr/don/en
Visit the World Health Organization's website to find out about the latest disease outbreaks around the world. You can also search their archives to learn about diseases that have appeared in particular years or countries.

Topics to research

- Tuberculosis is not a new disease – it was common in ancient Egypt, Greece, and Rome. Find out about evidence of the disease in the past and how our understanding of the causes and how it passes from person to person have changed through the centuries. Also, find out about the range of cures for the disease people have used, from bathing in urine (wee) to taking mountain air.

- Learn about vaccination and vaccines. Who invented the principle of vaccination? What diseases have been eradicated or transformed by vaccination programmes in different countries or globally? What vaccinations have you had and why?

- Infectious diseases kill millions of people every year but some are less well known than TB or malaria. Research one or more of the following: leishmaniasis, Chagas disease, leprosy, ebola, African sleeping sickness, Lume disease. In each case, identify the type of pathogen responsible, whether it spreads in the air or via a living thing, and its effects on people.

- Imagine you are responsible for educating a community about the dangers of a fictional infectious disease caused by a pathogen. Design a poster, video, or website informing people about the pathogen, the health problems it causes, and how they can help to reduce the danger or prevent its spread. Choose illustrations and slogans to get your message across simply and effectively.

Index